WHO AM I TO THINK I CAN CHANGE THE WORLD

I AM ME

WHO AM I TO THINK I CAN CHANGE THE WORLD — I AM ME.

I AM ME

TO CHANGE THE WORLD. A PHRASE EASILY SAID, BUT HOW EASILY CAN IT BE DONE?

Who are you to think you can change the world? It is not about who you know, it is about who you are. People often forget that those who change the world started out like everyone else. Their fate was not decided the day they were born, they created it themselves. The way we speak to ourselves is the way we will impact the world. If we are not willing to try and encourage ourselves, how are we going to support others? People who have changed the world have done some marvelous things, all of them different. Yet though their intentions were all different their mindsets were the same. Each world changer has a set of qualities.

WHO AM I TO THINK I CAN CHANGE THE WORLD

THESE QUALITIES CREATE, INSPIRE, ENCOURAGE, AND GROW THE CHANGE YOU ARE LOOKING FOR.

In order for you to change the world for the better, the better has to be inside you. Your passion, courage, and motivation are a few of the many qualities needed in today's society. Changing the world does not have to be a worldwide known show either, change can start with a simple whisper of words. A moment of silence, a small protest in respect. If you truly think you can change the world. You will.

The first step to understanding how capable you are, is an understanding that everything you do is in your control. That growing up and being heard does not have a set age or maturity. It is shown by who and what you are. Whenever you are ready, the world is waiting.

I AM ME

SOPHIA WAS A SHY, LOW SELF-ESTEEM AND NOT WELL LIKED GIRL HO HAD PERFECT ATTENDANCE AT SCHOOL BUT HAD AN IMPERFECT LIFE. WHO IS SHE TO THE THINK SHE COULD CHANGE THE WORLD?

I am me. Sophia could feel her heart beating faster the more she thought about the way the harsh words just fell out the mouths of those in the class. The insults, the ridicule, the hate. It had always been like that and there was nothing anyone could do to change it. She was told that when she grew older she could do anything, that she could choose the path her life wanted to go. Yet when would that be? When would she finally "grow" older? Would there be an announcement? Would she just feel it? Everything had been set out in front of her until now, when would all that end? Sophia watched her friends and family fade into the background and weaken to these same words. The same words and treatment that her past had suffered from her grandparents and even before then. When was that cycle truly going to end? Was it going to just happen one day? Sophia could feel her heart cracking with each shout and cry of hate, where was the happiness she was promised.

The names were being called at her now. The names only given to those with her chestnut colored skin.

“Stop it.” Sophia said. She could feel the fire inside her, the rage that no matter what she did it would not change their words nor the color of her skin.

School was supposed to teach and help her learn about the adult world, yet it was not anything like that.

How was that life? Where was her life going to take her? Where were the words going to take her? Sophia had to make a decision, she had to decide who was in control. Them, or her. The only thing holding Sophia down was the recurring thought of. **I am me**. A thought she had started to remind herself of on a daily basis. She could not change the color of her skin, and why would she?

WHO AM I TO THINK I CAN CHANGE THE WORLD

Sophia

I AM ME

Yet all the while the world would do nothing to stop the people around her from thinking she could.

This is where her story was going to change, this is where she was going to prove what one person could do.

"Who am I to think I can change the world?" She whispered.

"Who am I to think I cannot?" Sophia whispered again.

The world changes, yet it all had to start somewhere. Perhaps with someone, and if no one was going to help Sophia perhaps she could help herself.

It all started with confidence. She had to first remind herself that until she could show the world she had to show herself.

I AM ME

"I AM BEAUTIFUL. I AM PERFECT. I CAN CHANGE THE WORLD."

CONFIDENCE. COURAGE. DETERMINATION.

Every rock thrown into the water will make a splash, no matter the size of the pebble. With courage surrounding her heart she leaped at the first opportunity she could. To speak in front of the school, to let her voice be heard. She sang, shouted, cried her words out to share the truth and pain she felt. Sophia knew people would listen, but she also knew people would not.

DETERMINATION.

For this Sophia found another voice. Emma. A girl who shared the same passion as she did, and with that her "pebble" of an idea grew bigger. Those around her began to follow, it started at one voice but turned into two, then four, then eight, then twelve. Though the true determination was not standing back when trouble came.

WHO AM I TO THINK I CAN CHANGE THE WORLD

"WHO ARE YOU TO THINK YOU CAN CHANGE THE WORLD!" SOMEONE SHOUTED AT HER.

I AM ME

Emma saw this. A girl who dreamed of someday sitting in a politic seat, something that many her age did not want to pursue. She was a girl, she was young, she was nonassertive, nor popular. When was the right time for someone to start listening to her? If she had ideas, when was the time to share them?

Schools are losing children every week. A country that thrives on protection but can't protect those who need it most. Emma was tired of it, she was tired of seeing students who would no longer be able to pursue their dreams like her. A gun in a school held by someone with hate in their heart. Taking the lives of children whose dreams were stopped before they had even begun.

I AM ME

WHO AM I TO THINK I CAN CHANGE THE WORLD

In other countries she knew this was not the standard way. If someone were to bring a gun into a school, they would take them away because the country cared about the students. The people making the decisions are not students anymore, they do not know what it was like to wake up every morning worried about what might happen that day. They were adults who could choose where and what they wanted to do, if the children were forced to go to school then people should be forced to do something about it. The only people who could convince the world were the ones living in the danger, Students. Emma was a frail skinny girl with curly brown hair, she blended into the crowd and was invisible amongst her peers. Even if she wanted to do something, could she?

"Who am I to think I can change the world?" Emma sighed.

"Who am I to think I cannot." She felt her heart beat faster.

Voices are meant to be heard. No matter how soft or silent they still make a sound. Emma was sick of hearing the

I AM ME

names of the people she would never see grow up. Each name broke her heart piece by piece, if she did not do something there would be nothing left to break. Gun control was a political issue, it was something she felt passionate about and if she wanted to make a change, she had to show it too.

INSPIRED. STRONG LEADERSHIP. CREATIVITY.

It was easy for her to feel the inspiration around her. The students who were also saddened by the way they no longer felt safe in school. This was her moment to show them Leadership where there was none. A small frail brown-eyed girl who wanted nothing more than to feel safe while she learned about her culture and home. There should not even be a right for basic safety, but there was, and she planned to lead it out.

Getting herself heard called for the most creative tasks. People only learned and listened to the social media around them. She would surround herself with those who would

WHO AM I TO THINK I CAN CHANGE THE WORLD

listen and spread her words on every platform she could reach. Her closest friend Lucas watched with wide-eyes as more and more people grew aware. He was part of her cause and because of that Emma would bring people together from all across the country who had the same goals in mind. They would rally together and although they would be crossed with obstacles. A blockade can only stand when it is matched with equal weight. If the army for guns was prepared to defend, her brigade of peace would be more massive. It would be stronger, and it would never ever surrender

"WHO ARE YOU TO THINK YOU CAN CHANGE THE WORLD." SOMEONE SHOUTED.

"I AM ME!" EMMA SHOUTED BACK.

Lucas watched in amazement as a girl he had never spoken to or even heard from was letting her voice be shouted from the rooftops. Is it possible for someone to start from nothing and end with a better world? Lucas would never have believed it. He had watched too many people try and fail, even he has tried before. The only people who can make their dreams come true are the ones with money to spare. His family had barely enough as it was. Living under the poverty line was something he was so ashamed to believe at first. He did not understand how it was possible either. He rarely saw his mother as she spent every waking moment of her day working for others. She would come home and care for him and his siblings and not once has he heard her complain. His father worked just as hard, he would leave for weeks at a time just to provide enough housing and food to make their bellies full.

Yet what would happen the day one of his siblings breaks an arm. Or his mother gets sick and cannot work. He was already given reduced price lunches and unless he had money and fancy clothes, no one was going to listen to him.

WHO AM I TO THINK I CAN CHANGE THE WORLD

Lucas

I AM ME

"WHO AM I TO THINK I CAN CHANGE THE WORLD?"
HE ROLLED HIS EYES.

"WHO AM I TO THINK I CANNOT."
HE STARTED THINKING ABOUT
WHAT A LITTLE CHANGE MIGHT DO.

WHERE WAS HE GOING TO START?

COMPASSION. TRUTH. ASPIRATION

The first step was to bring the people in through compassion. He would not beg or ask for money, but instead he would shout and strive for sick leave, strive for health insurance, he would fight for higher wages. Whatever he could do to show his parents that their hard work is paying off. No matter how wealthy someone is however, everyone was built the same. Everyone had a heart.

Lucas would use that compassion to share the bare truth of what life was like. One of the biggest problems his country faced was that people did not know. No one wanted to hear about the pain and suffering, only the good. It is like a bad

WHO AM I TO THINK I CAN CHANGE THE WORLD

wound on an arm, most people would cover it with a bandaid. Yet Lucas was going to be the one to rip it off.

The ones who are blocked behind debt and work are the ones that need their voices to be heard the most. Lucas would set his aspirations high, but still achievable. The best direction of any goal is to make it achievable, once that is complete another goal will take its place. He used what available resources he could, the free use of the internet, and more. The one thing that will never cost however is conversation. He knew one of his goals was to have a conversation with someone who was not like him. Someone who had never gone a day without a meal or a winter without a blanket. These were the types of people he needed to show, to open their eyes to the wound under the bandage.

Of course, however there would be doubt. There would be those who have lived so poorly they no longer believe in steady living. The constant fear and worry about when they

I AM ME

WILL EAT NEXT HAS NOW BECOME NOTHING MORE THAN A HABIT FOR THEM.

HO ARE YOU TO THINK YOU CAN CHANGE THE WORLD?" SOMEONE QUESTIONED.

I AM ME

There are numerous qualities for world-changers. Some have them all, some have a few, but something you will never find in the successful, something you will never find in the world changers, is fear. There are changes happening all around us, many people often reject an idea of change because breaking the chain of "normal" can cause tension and fear.

Fear is everywhere, it is like an invisible virus that is meant to contain and erase all thoughts or attempts at change. It eats away with the weak minded, it chews and spits out those who are willing to bend to it. There are more people who fear than those who do not, this is why things do not change.

WHO AM I TO THINK I CAN CHANGE THE WORLD

It takes a powerful soul to combat the plague of fear. The things to remember that it is just fear. It is something that can be fixed, healed, and revealed. Like a child afraid of the dark. It starts with the door left wide open, the hall light shining inside the room revealing everything as it is. You have to reveal what is causing the fear, to understand the dark we first have to see it. To understand the change, we first have to see where it is. That is where you, the worldchanger comes in. Many of us are blind to our own fear, we are blind to the change that is needed because we do not see it. Who controls your fear? Is it you? Or fear itself. Along with the dozens of qualities a world-changer has, there are also the ones they do not. Remind yourself who controls your fear. What could you accomplish if you were not afraid (fear) or the fear of failing?

The road to success, the path to change the world, all goals start with nothing more than an idea. The way you form and build that idea is what will define the change. No one was

I AM ME

born with a famous or well known name, it was their actions that defined their remembrance. If you want to change the world it starts within you.

Change starts with Confidence.

Change continues with Courage.

Change thrives on Determination.

Change builds with Inspiration.

Change solidifies under Strong Leadership.

Change is remembered through Creativity.

Change grows through Compassion.

Change is made with the Truth.

Change is a never-ending Aspiration.

To be the person who changes the world you must remember where this change first started from. The pebble of an idea in your mind. If you do not believe you can change the world how will anyone else?.

WHO AM I TO THINK I CAN CHANGE THE WORLD

CHANGE STARTS WITHIN YOU

You

MUST

be the

CHANGE

You wish to see

IN THE

world.

×

I AM ME

"If you don't like something, change it, if you can't change it, change your attitude"

Maya Angelou

WHO AM I TO THINK I CAN CHANGE THE WORLD

I AM ME

I AM ME

You have the right to change your life for the better.

No matter how grown you may be, you were given a voice for a reason.

You can change the world too.

You can show confidence, courage, determination through your actions.

You can show inspiration, leadership, and creativity through your voice.

You can show compassion, truth, and aspiration through your heart.

You too can change the world.

NOW IT TIME TO PROVE IT.

WHO AM I TO THINK
I CAN CHANGE
THE WORLD

CONFIDENCE
COURAGE
DETERMINATION
INSPIRATION
CREATIVITY
ACTIONS

YOU TOO CAN CHANGE THE WORLD

I AM ME

QUESTIONS:

Who am I to think I can change the world?

What qualities do I have that can change the world?

Who controls my fear?

Where does my change start?

Who could I relate most with in this story?

WHO AM I TO THINK I CAN CHANGE THE WORLD

YOUR WORD CAN CHANGE THE WORLD

CPSIA information can be obtained
at www.ICGtesting.com
Printed in the USA
BVHW020840230522
637748BV00039BA/25

9 781087 995212

Above Atlantic Canada

Aerial Photography by Russ Heinl

NIMBUS PUBLISHING

Nimbus Publishing Limited
PO Box 9301, Station A
Halifax, NS B3K 5N5
(902)455-4286

Design: Graphic Detail, Charlottetown, PEI
Front cover image: The Confederation Bridge,
linking PEI and New Brunswick (see page 82).
Back cover image: Lunenburg's waterfront (see page 66).
Printed and bound in Canada

All images by Russ Heinl except for
iv, 16, 17, 41, 46-47, 50, 51, 54-55,
which are by Barrett and MacKay
P.O. Box 384, Cornwall, PEI, C0A 1H0

Canadian Cataloguing in Publication Data
Heinl, Russ, 1949-
ISBN 1-55109-322-7

1. Atlantic Provinces – Aerial photographs I. Title.
2. FC2004.H44 2000 917.15'0022'2 C99-950252-2
3. F1035.8.H44 2000

Canada

Nimbus Publishing acknowledges financial support for its publishing activities from the Government of Canada through the Book Publishing Industry Development Program (BPIDP), and the Canada Council.

Russ Heinl's images are available from:

Image Network Inc.
16 East 3rd Avenue Vancouver, BC, Canada V5T 1C3
Phone: (604) 879-2533 Fax: (604) 879-1290
e-mail: info@imagenetworkinc.com

The cameras used for the photography in this book were a pair of Nikon F-5s supported by the following Nikon lenses: 16 mm f2.8 fish eye; 20/35 mm f2.8; 35/70 mm f2.8; 80/200 mm f2.8; 300 mm f2.8 and two teleconverters taking the 300 mm up to 420 mm and 600 mm when required.

For Matthew, the finest son
a father could wish for.

FOREWORD

FACING PAGE: SUMMER BOATING ON THE CHEBOGUE RIVER, NOVA SCOTIA.

I consider myself privileged that my work as an aerial photographer has taken me to some of the most fascinating and visually captivating places in the world: Europe, Alaska, America, and over almost all of Canada. Having said that, I must confess that as a seasoned aerial traveller, the haunting beauty of the Atlantic provinces caught me totally off guard.

The pristine wilderness of "The Rock," as Newfoundland is affectionately called, reminded me of the famed Norwegian-like fjords of Canada's own West Coast. Mother Nature has equally blessed Prince Edward Island with the most vibrant of artist's palettes. Where else could a photographer find such a tantalizing mix of rust red earth tones and lush verdant landscapes suspended in a sea of emerald green, thoughtfully framed by an unending deep blue sky?

This photographic journey continued unrelentingly over New Brunswick and Nova Scotia, often jumping between provincial borders when logistics and local weather patterns dictated. The unique beauty of New Brunswick's Hopewell Rocks was only further enhanced when viewed alongside the grand majesty of Nova Scotia's Cape Breton Highlands National Park. A powerful sense of history unfolded below as we photographed some of the oldest forts and spectacular architecture Canada has to offer. Throughout our flights, we repeatedly discovered the quintessence of the quaint coastal fishing villages was like that of randomly scattered jewels concealed along the rugged coastlines of both provinces.

Aerial photography is an unforgiving discipline. Not only because a shot may be lost forever due to a miscalculation on the photographer's part, but also in the physical sense. We fly with our helicopter doors removed or slid open in harsh environments. At times we fly at breakneck speeds a few feet off the deck, or back our helicopter into a steep canyon wall, our tailrotor a mere stone's throw from the granite cliff face, just to get the right angle on that "must have" shot. Sub-zero temperatures, violent mountain turbulence, and oxygen concerns are, for us, the "norm."

To shoot the Atlantic provinces, two types of helicopters were employed. The beautifully smooth, fast, and powerful A-Star AS-350s were pressed into service when long range or more technically difficult missions called for it. For the other flights, our aerial platform of choice was the venerable Bell 206 Jet Ranger, our tried, trusted, and true workhorse.

The helicopter affords me the three-dimensional control I require to capture on film not only the grand sweeping landscapes that are so often the hallmark of aerial work, but also the ability to "ground" the viewer by becoming closer and more intimate to my chosen subject.

ONE OF NOVA SCOTIA'S MOST PICTURESQUE AND HISTORICALLY IMPORTANT TOWNS, IN 1995 THE UNITED NATIONS DECLARED LUNENBURG A WORLD HERITAGE SITE.

LUNENBURG, NOVA SCOTIA

Helicopters are vibrating, shaking aerial platforms definitely not agreeable to cameras, which prefer to be held with rock-solid stability. To overcome this, I fly with a pair of heavy-duty tungsten-wheeled gyro stabilizers. The gyros are attached to the camera's body and although they are back-breakingly heavy, they permit the use of slow speed films, slow shutter speeds, and long lenses in the helicopters.

I should like to comment that none of my images have been enhanced nor have any filters been used on the lenses except for circular polarizers, which are on most of the time.

The Atlantic region has been captured well by many capable photographers before me. I hope, however, that these unique aerial portraits of such a famous and endearing Canadian landscape will ignite the adventurer in you as you join me on this aerial journey high above the Atlantic provinces.

FROM OVER THE SAINT JOHN RIVER, THE WESTMORLAND STREET BRIDGE LEADS TRAFFIC INTO FREDERICTON.

FREDERICTON, NEW BRUNSWICK

PEI

ROLLING FARMLANDS IN PEI FORM ONE OF THE ISLAND'S MOST DISTINCTIVE IMAGES.

FACING PAGE: NEAR BORDEN, PEI, WHERE THE RED SANDSTONE SHORELINE STRETCHES INTO THE HORIZON.

CAPE SPEAR, IN NEWFOUNDLAND'S AVALON REGION, IS NORTH AMERICA'S EASTERNMOST POINT.

CAPE SPEAR, NEWFOUNDLAND

L'ANSE AUX MEADOWS, NEWFOUNDLAND

AT THE TIP OF NEWFOUNDLAND'S GREAT NORTHERN PENINSULA, L'ANSE AUX MEADOWS IS THE ONLY AUTHENTICATED NORSE SITE IN THE NEW WORLD; THE VIKINGS ESTABLISHED THE VERY FIRST EUROPEAN SETTLEMENT IN NORTH AMERICA HERE IN APPROXIMATELY 1000 A.D.

GRAND MANAN ISLAND, NEW BRUNSWICK

SUCCESSFUL EFFORTS AT AQUACULTURE ON GRAND MANAN INCLUDE THE PRODUCTION OF SALMON AND TROUT IN THE CAGES SEEN HERE.

CAVENDISH, PEI

NEAR CAVENDISH, THE UNMISTAKABLE RED CLAY ROADS OF PEI LIE IN STRIKING CONTRAST TO THE LUSH FIELDS.

FACING PAGE: ST. PETER'S HARBOUR, PEI. THE SQUARE TOWER OF THE ST. PETER'S LIGHTHOUSE IS LOCATED ON THE OCEAN SIDE OF A LAGOON. THE LIGHTHOUSES FOUND THROUGHOUT PEI ARE CAREFULLY PRESERVED REMINDERS OF THE ISLAND'S SEAFARING HISTORY.

LOCATED IN THE CAPE BRETON HIGHLANDS NATIONAL PARK, THE KELTIC LODGE IS ONE OF THE AREA'S MOST POPULAR RESORTS.

INGONISH, NOVA SCOTIA

CAPE BRETON, NOVA SCOTIA

THE RUGGED COASTLINE OF CAPE BRETON ISLAND PROVIDES SOME OF NOVA SCOTIA'S MOST DRAMATIC SCENERY.

OVERLEAF: BRIER ISLAND, NOVA SCOTIA. THE MARITIMES IS ONE OF THE WORLD'S BEST WHALE-WATCHING AREAS WHERE OVER TEN TYPES OF WHALES CAN BE SPOTTED IN ITS WATERS.

FREDERICTON, NEW BRUNSWICK

CHRIST CHURCH CATHEDRAL, CONSECRATED IN 1853, WAS BUILT FROM STONE TAKEN FROM SOUTHERN NEW BRUNSWICK'S GRINDSTONE ISLAND. THE CHURCH WAS NORTH AMERICA'S FIRST EXAMPLE OF THE GOTHIC REVIVAL STYLE OF ARCHITECTURE.

FACING PAGE: FREDERICTON'S CITY HALL WAS BUILT IN 1876 AND IS A CLASSIC MODEL OF NINETEENTH-CENTURY CIVIC ARCHITECTURE.

GRAND MANAN ISLAND, NEW BRUNSWICK

THE STEEP CLIFFS OF GRAND MANAN ISLAND, LOCATED ON THE BAY OF FUNDY, SHOW 900-MILLION-YEAR-OLD SEDIMENTARY ROCK.

BUCTOUCHE, NEW BRUNSWICK

BUCTOUCHE, ON THE NORTHUMBERLAND STRAIT, BECAME THE HOME TO NUMEROUS ACADIAN FAMILIES RETURNING FROM EXILE, AFTER THEIR EXPULSION BY THE BRITISH IN 1755.

PEGGY'S COVE, ONE OF NOVA SCOTIA'S MOST RECOGNIZABLE SITES, IS HOME TO THE FISHERMAN'S MONUMENT CREATED BY ARTIST, WILLIAM DEGARTHE. A MORE RECENT MONUMENT IN NEARBY WHALESBACK MARKS THE TRAGEDY OF THE 1998 SWISS AIR DISASTER OFF PEGGY'S COVE.

PEGGY'S COVE, NOVA SCOTIA

HALIFAX, NOVA SCOTIA

THE HALIFAX WATERFRONT IS A POPULAR SUMMERTIME DESTINATION, WHERE EIGHTEENTH-CENTURY BUILDINGS STAND SIDE-BY-SIDE MODERN BUSINESSES AND DEVELOPMENTS.

PORT AU CHOIX IS THE HOME TO TWO MAJOR ARCHAEOLOGICAL SITES, ONE OF WHICH CONSISTS OF DORSET INUIT ARTIFACTS FROM BETWEEN 200 AND 600 A.D.; THE OTHER, A LARGE CEMETERY DATING FROM BETWEEN 2000 AND 1200 B.C.

PORT AU CHOIX, NEWFOUNDLAND

A NEWFOUNDLAND MOOSE

FIRST INTRODUCED TO NEWFOUNDLAND IN 1878, THERE ARE NOW APPROXIMATELY 50,000 MOOSE IN THE PROVINCE.

GROS MORNE NATIONAL PARK, NEWFOUNDLAND

A UNITED NATIONS WORLD HERITAGE SITE, GROS MORNE NATIONAL PARK ENCOMPASSES SPECTACULAR FJORDS, MOUNTAINOUS PEAKS AND PLATEAUS, AND GEOLOGICAL WONDERS.

NOW A LEADING TOURIST SITE, THE IMPRESSIVE STAR-SHAPED CITADEL WAS ONE OF NORTH AMERICA'S LARGEST BRITISH FORTRESSES. BUILT BETWEEN 1828 AND 1856, IT PROVIDED AN EXCELLENT VANTAGE POINT FROM WHICH THE CITY AND HARBOUR COULD BE VIEWED.

HALIFAX, NOVA SCOTIA

YARMOUTH, NOVA SCOTIA

BOATS DOT THE WATERS OUTSIDE YARMOUTH'S NEWLY REJUVENATED HARBOURFRONT.

ALTHOUGH STILL OPERATIONAL AS A COAST GUARD LIGHT, THE LIGHTHOUSE AT WEST POINT HAS BEEN CONVERTED INTO A NINE-ROOM INN.

WEST POINT, PEI

PEI

ON THE NORTHERN COAST OF PEI, EXPANSIVE BEACHES AND TEMPTING BLUE WATERS BECKON VISITORS AND RESIDENTS ALL SUMMER LONG.

ONCE THE CENTRE OF THE SIXTEENTH-CENTURY BASQUE WHALING STATIONS, PORT AUX BASQUES IS NOW NEWFOUNDLAND'S PRINCIPAL GATEWAY PORT, AND HOME TO THE PROVINCE'S LARGEST FERRY TERMINAL.

PORT AUX BASQUES, NEWFOUNDLAND

PORT AUX BASQUES, NEWFOUNDLAND

PORT AUX BASQUES IS ONE OF TWO POINTS OF ARRIVAL AND DEPARTURE FOR THE MORE THAN 420,000 FERRY PASSENGERS TRAVELLING BETWEEN NOVA SCOTIA AND NEWFOUNDLAND EACH YEAR.

YARMOUTH BAR, NOVA SCOTIA

GOLDEN HUES ENGULF YARMOUTH BAR AS DUSK FALLS.

KOUCHIBOUGUAC NATIONAL PARK ATTRACTS BEACH-GOERS, CYCLISTS, HIKERS, AND CAMPERS.

KOUCHIBOUGUAC NATIONAL PARK, NEW BRUNSWICK

GRAND MANAN ISLAND, NEW BRUNSWICK

HERE, APPROPRIATELY, IS A BIRD'S-EYE VIEW OF GRAND MANAN ISLAND, WHICH IS LOCATED ON THE EASTERN FLYWAY FOR OVER FOUR HUNDRED SPECIES OF MIGRATORY BIRDS.

NEAR DARLING LAKE, YARMOUTH COUNTY

SPARKLING WATERS FRAME A CHURCH AND CEMETERY, NEAR DARLING LAKE, IN YARMOUTH COUNTY.

FACING PAGE: APPLE-GROWING IN THE ANNAPOLIS VALLEY HAS A LONG HISTORY, WITH A CENSUS FROM 1698 REPORTING THAT IN ANNAPOLIS ROYAL ALONE THERE WERE OVER 1,584 APPLE TREES.

ST. JOHN'S, NEWFOUNDLAND

COLOURFUL HOUSES MARK THE LANDSCAPE IN ST. JOHN'S.

FACING PAGE: NEWFOUNDLAND'S TABLELANDS WITH THEIR DISTINCTIVE FEATURES OF BARREN YELLOW GRANITE AND BEYOND, THICKLY GROWING EVERGREENS.

THE CAT
BAY ferries

YARMOUTH HAS LONG BEEN A BUSY PORT FOR CANADIAN AND U.S. TRAVELLERS. *THE CAT,* SHOWN HERE LEAVING YARMOUTH, IS A HIGH-SPEED CATAMARAN THAT REACHES BAR HARBOUR, MAINE IN LESS THAN THREE HOURS.

WITH ITS ONCE CELEBRATED HARBOUR AND HISTORIC FORTRESS, LOUISBOURG CONTINUES TO EDUCATE VISITORS ABOUT LIFE AS IT WAS IN THE FRENCH MILITARY TOWN.

LOUISBOURG, NOVA SCOTIA

LUNENBURG, NOVA SCOTIA

DURING THE SUMMER MONTHS, TOURISTS FLOCK TO THIS HISTORIC SEAFARING TOWN TO TAKE IN THE SIGHTS AND VISIT POPULAR LOBSTER RESTAURANTS SUCH AS THIS ONE.

SPECTACULARLY RUGGED, SOME OF NEW BRUNSWICK'S COASTS ARE RECORDED AS BEING 350 MILLION YEARS OLD.

GRAND MANAN ISLAND, NEW BRUNSWICK

CAMPOBELLO ISLAND, NEW BRUNSWICK

FAMOUS AS THE SUMMER HOME OF AMERICAN PRESIDENT, FRANKLIN D. ROOSEVELT, CAMPOBELLO ISLAND IS ALSO NOTABLE FOR ITS ACTIVE FISHING COMMUNITY.

THE STRIKING LANDSCAPE OF INGONISH IS PUNCTUATED BY ITS LOCATION BETWEEN TWO BAYS, WITH MIDDLE HEAD PENINSULA SEPARATING THE PAIR.

INGONISH, NOVA SCOTIA

HALIFAX, NOVA SCOTIA

POPULAR SUMMER ENTERTAINMENT ON THE HALIFAX WATERFRONT INCLUDES THE INTERNATIONAL BUSKERS' FESTIVAL, WHICH TAKES PLACE EVERY AUGUST.

OVERLEAF: CREATING AN APPEALING PATTERN OF COLOUR AND TEXTURE, A PEI FARMER TENDS TO HIS LAND.

DRAMATIC SCENERY OF LAND MEETING SEA IS A HALLMARK OF NEWFOUNDLAND'S LANDSCAPE.

TWILLINGATE, NEWFOUNDLAND

GRAND BRUIT, NEWFOUNDLAND

AN ISOLATED COMMUNITY ON NEWFOUNDLAND'S SOUTH COAST, GRAND BRUIT LIES CLOSE TO A 305-METRE-HIGH CLIFF OVER WHICH THE SOUND GENERATED BY FALLING WATER GAVE THIS HAMLET ITS FRENCH NAME: GRAND BRUIT MEANING "GREAT NOISE."

LUNENBURG, NOVA SCOTIA

LUNENBURG'S FISHERIES MUSEUM OF THE ATLANTIC HAS THE PROVINCE'S LARGEST MUSEUM COLLECTION DEDICATED TO THE FISHERY.

LOUISBOURG, NOVA SCOTIA

LOBSTER TRAPS LINE THE WATERFRONT IN LOUISBOURG.

OVERLEAF: HOPEWELL CAPE, NEW BRUNSWICK. WHEN TIDE IS LOW, THE HOPEWELL ROCKS HAVE BEEN DESCRIBED AS LOOKING LIKE GIANT FLOWER VASES.

THOUGH IT RECENTLY LOST ITS TRUNK, ELEPHANT ROCK REMAINS A FIXTURE ON THE BEACHSIDE NEAR NORTH CAPE.

NEAR NORTH CAPE, PEI

NORTH CAPE, PEI

THIS LIGHTHOUSE WARNS SHIPS TO AVOID THE ONE-AND-A-HALF KILOMETRE-LONG ROCKY REEF THAT JUTS OUT FROM NORTH CAPE.

BURGEO, NEWFOUNDLAND

BRILLIANT SHADES OF GREEN AND BLUE STRETCH OUT NEAR BURGEO, NEWFOUNDLAND.

CHARLOTTETOWN RETAINS ITS EIGHTEENTH-CENTURY LAYOUT, MAKING IT AN IDEAL CITY TO EXPLORE ON FOOT.

CHARLOTTETOWN, PEI

DRIVERS CAN CROSS THE CONFEDERATION BRIDGE, LINKING NEW BRUNSWICK AND PEI, IN JUST TWELVE MINUTES.

CONFEDERATION BRIDGE, FROM THE NEW BRUNSWICK SIDE

ANNAPOLIS VALLEY, NOVA SCOTIA

FACING PAGE AND LEFT: CONTRASTING LOOKS AT THE LANDSCAPE OF NOVA SCOTIA'S ANNAPOLIS VALLEY.

LOCATED ON THE EASTERN SHORE OF THE NORTHUMBERLAND STRAIT, KOUCHIBOUGUAC NATIONAL PARK IS HOME TO MANY ENDANGERED PIPING PLOVERS.

KOUCHIBOUGUAC NATIONAL PARK, NEW BRUNSWICK

GRAND MANAN ISLAND, NEW BRUNSWICK

GRAND MANAN'S FISHING INDUSTRY IS KNOWN FOR ITS CATCH OF SALMON, SARDINES, LOBSTER, AND HERRING.

OVERLEAF: SHALLOW BOGS AND ABUNDANT VEGETATION CHARACTERIZE THE SOUTH COAST OF NEWFOUNDLAND.

THE CONFEDERATION BRIDGE

STRETCHING MORE THAN TWELVE KILOMETRES, THE CONFEDERATION BRIDGE OPENED TO GREAT FANFARE ON MAY 31, 1997.

NORTH CAPE, PEI

THE CLEAR WATERS OF PEI'S NORTH CAPE REEF ATTRACT EVEN THOSE WITHOUT SWIMMING SUITS.

ST. JOHN'S, NEWFOUNDLAND

A VIEW OF CABOT TOWER BUILT BETWEEN 1898 AND 1900 IN HONOUR OF BOTH THE 400th ANNIVERSARY OF JOHN CABOT'S ARRIVAL AND QUEEN VICTORIA'S DIAMOND JUBILEE.

THE ARCHES, NEWFOUNDLAND

THE ARCHES, FOUND ON NEWFOUNDLAND'S GREAT NORTHERN PENINSULA.

CAPE BRETON, NOVA SCOTIA

THE CABOT TRAIL, WHICH WINDS THROUGH THE BEAUTIFULLY RUGGED TERRAIN OF CAPE BRETON'S NORTHERN SHORE, OFFERS ONE OF THE WORLD'S MOST SCENIC DRIVES.

WATER AND GRANITE—NEWFOUNDLAND'S DEFINING NATURAL FEATURES—FORM A STRIKING WATERFALL.

SOUTH COAST OF NEWFOUNDLAND, NEAR BURGEO